Mabel Borton Beebe

The Story of Oliver Hazard Perry for young Readers

Mabel Borton Beebe

The Story of Oliver Hazard Perry for young Readers

ISBN/EAN: 9783743338753

Manufactured in Europe, USA, Canada, Australia, Japa

Cover: Foto ©ninafisch / pixelio.de

Manufactured and distributed by brebook publishing software
(www.brebook.com)

Mabel Borton Beebe

The Story of Oliver Hazard Perry for young Readers

CONTENTS.

THE STORY OF OLIVER HAZARD PERRY

I.—How the Perry Family Came to Rhode Island.

A very long time ago, there lived in England a young Quaker whose name was Edmund Perry.

At that time the Quakers were much persecuted. They were a quiet and peace-loving people, and would not serve in the army. They had their own religious meetings, and refused to pay money for the support of the Church of England. For these reasons, they were imprisoned, beaten, and driven from their homes.

Edmund Perry believed that the Quakers were right, and he could not endure these persecutions. So, in 1650, he came to America to live.

Thirty years before that time, a company of Pilgrims had left England because they also wished to be free to worship God as they chose.

They had founded a colony at Plymouth, which is now in the state of Massachusetts.

Edmund Perry thought that in this settlement of Pilgrims he could surely live peaceably in the enjoyment of his own belief. He did not stay long in Plymouth, however. His Quaker religion was hated there, as it had been in England; and the Pilgrims did not wish to have any one in their colony who did not agree with them.

Not far from Plymouth was the colony of Rhode Island, which had been founded by Roger Williams. Roger Williams declared that a man is responsible for his opinions only to God and his own conscience, and that no one has any right to punish him for his belief.

The people in the Rhode Island colony did not quarrel with one another about religion, but lived together in peace.

Edmund Perry thought that this was the place where he could make a home for himself and his family. He therefore purchased a large tract of land on the shores of Narragansett Bay, near what is now the site of South Kingston.

Here he lived for the rest of his life, at peace with all about him, even his Indian neighbors. His descendants also lived in this neighborhood. Among them were judges, lawyers, and doctors, as well as farmers and mechanics; and they were always highly respected in the colony.

Christopher Raymond Perry, a great-great-grandson of Edmund Perry, was born in December, 1761.

At that time there were thirteen colonies or great settlements of English people at different places along the Atlantic coast of what is now the United States. But troubles had already begun to brew between the people of these colonies and the king of England. These troubles finally led to the Revolutionary War.

Christopher Perry, although a mere boy, was one of the first persons in Rhode Island to offer himself for this war. He joined a company of volunteers known as the "Kingston Reds"; but soon afterwards left the army and entered the navy. Here he served, having many adventures, until the close of the war, in 1783.

He had become very fond of a sailor's life, and when there was no more use for him in the navy he obtained a place on a merchant vessel, and went on a cruise to Ireland.

During the homeward voyage he became acquainted with one of the passengers, a beautiful girl of Scotch descent, whose name was Sara Alexander. Soon after their arrival in America, their friendship ripened into love, and in 1784 they were married in Philadelphia.

Christopher Perry, though but twenty-three years of age, was then the captain of a vessel. The young couple went to live with Christopher's father, on the old Perry estate in South Kingston.

This was then a farm of two hundred acres. The old homestead stood at the foot of a hill not far from the Narragansett shore.

Through the trees in a neighboring wood, shone the white stones which marked the graves of the Quaker, Edmund Perry, and many of his children and grandchildren.

The Perry family were glad to welcome Christopher's young wife into their home. She was as intelligent as she was beautiful; and her sweet and happy disposition made every one love her.

Christopher Perry gave up his life on the sea for a time, and many happy months were spent in the old home.

On the 23d of August, 1785, their first baby boy was born. He was named for an uncle and a great-great-grandfather, Oliver Hazard Perry.

II.—SCHOOL DAYS.

Oliver was a winsome baby and he grew strong and beautiful very fast. Every one loved him, for he thought all strangers were friends, and was never afraid of them.

Indeed he was not afraid of anything, for to him there was no danger. We shall see that he kept this same fearlessness all through his life.

When he was three years old, he was playing one day with an older child, in the road near his grandfather's house. A man was seen coming rapidly towards them on horseback. The elder child ran out of the way, calling to Oliver to do the same.

The little fellow sat quite still, however, until the horse was nearly upon him.   As the horseman

drew rein, Oliver looked up into his face and said, "Man, you will not ride over me, will you?"

The gentleman, who was a friend of the family's, carried him into the house, and told the story.

When scarcely more than a baby, Oliver sat

upon his mother's knee, while she taught him letters and words. It was not long before he could read quite well. By the time he was five years old, there were two other babies to keep the beautiful, loving mother busy. So it was thought best to send Oliver to school.

Not far from the Perrys', there lived an old gentleman whom the people loved because of his goodness of heart. As there was no school near by, he had often been asked to teach the neighborhood children.

The good old man was notoriously lazy, and consented upon one condition—that he should be allowed to have a bed in the schoolroom.

Teachers were few in those days, and, since there was no one else, the bed was set up. How amusing it must have been to see the children standing about the master's bed and reciting their lessons!

It was to this strange school that little Oliver was first sent. Some girl cousins lived on the adjoining farm. Though they were all older than he, it was Oliver's duty, each day, to take them to and from school. No one, not even the other scholars, thought this at all strange. His dignified manners always made him seem older than he really was.

One day his mother told him that he was old enough to go to school at Tower Hill, a place four miles away. Boys and girls would now think that a long way to go to school; but Oliver and his cousins did not mind the walk through the woods and over the hills.

The master of this school was so old that he had once taught Oliver's grandfather. He was not lazy, however, and was never known to lose his temper.

It was not long until a change was made and Oliver was taken away from "old master Kelly."

For several years past, Oliver's father had been again on the sea. He had commanded vessels on successful voyages to Europe and South America, and now he had a large income. He was therefore able to pay for better teaching for Oliver and the younger children.

So the family moved from South Kingston to Newport, a larger town, with better schools.

At first Oliver did not like the change. The discipline was much more strict than it had been in the little country schools.

His teacher, Mr. Frazer, had one serious fault. He had a violent temper which was not always controlled.

One day he became angry at Oliver and broke a ruler over his head. Without a word, Oliver took his hat and went home. He told his mother that he would never go back.

The wise mother said nothing until the next morning. Then, giving him a note for Mr. Frazer, she told him to go to school as usual. The proud boy's lip quivered and tears were in his eyes, but he never thought of disobeying his mother.

The note he carried was a kind one, telling Mr. Frazer that she intrusted Oliver to his care again and hoped that she would not have cause to regret it.

After this Oliver had no better friend than Mr. Frazer. On holidays they walked together to the seashore and spent many hours wandering along the beach. The schoolmaster took great delight in teaching Oliver the rules of navigation, and the use of the instruments necessary for sailing a vessel.

Oliver learned these things so readily that it was not long until Mr. Frazer said he was the best navigator in Rhode Island. This, of course, was not strictly true, but it showed what an apt scholar the boy was.

Oliver made many friends in Newport. Among them was the Frenchman, Count Rochambeau. The father of this man was a great general, and had once commanded some French troops who helped the Americans in the Revolutionary War.

Count Rochambeau often invited Oliver to dine with him, and one day he gave him a beautiful little watch.

When Oliver was twelve years old, his father gave up his life on the sea. The family then moved to Westerly, a little village in the southwestern part of Rhode Island.

For five years Oliver had been a faithful pupil of Mr. Frazer's, and he was now far advanced for his years.

III.—Plans for the Future.

About this time some unexpected troubles arose in our country.

France and England had been at war for years. The French were anxious that America should join in the quarrel; and when they could not bring this about by persuasion, they tried to use force.

French cruisers were sent to the American shores to capture merchant vessels while on their way to foreign ports.

You may be sure that this roused the people from one end of the United States to the other. Preparations for war with France were begun; and the first great need was a better navy.

At the close of the Revolutionary War, all work on government vessels had been stopped. Those that were unfinished were sold to shipping merchants. Even the ships of war that had done such good service, were sold to foreign countries. In this way, the entire American navy passed out of existence.

But now the President, John Adams, went to work to establish a navy that should give protection to American commerce.

In the spring of 1798, a naval department was organized, with Benjamin Stoddart as the first Secretary of the Navy. The following summer was busy with active preparations. Six new frigates were built, and to these were added a number of other vessels of various kinds.

Captain Christopher Perry was given command of one of the new frigates that were being built at Warren, a small town near Bristol, Rhode Island. This vessel was to be called the *General Greene.*

In order to superintend the building of this vessel, Captain Perry, with his wife, left his quiet home in Westerly, and went to stay in Warren.

Oliver, then not quite thirteen years old, remained at home to take charge of the family.

He saw that his sister and brothers went to school regularly. He bought all the family provisions. Each day he wrote to his father and mother, telling them about home affairs. In the meantime, he was busily planning what his work in life should be.

His mother had taught him that a man must be brave, and always ready to serve his country. She had told him many stories of battles fought long ago in her native land across the sea.

Oliver had lived most of his life in sight of the sea, and had spent many hours with seamen. It is not strange, therefore, that he should decide,—" I wish to be a captain like my father."

He had heard of the troubles with France, and he longed to help defend his country. And so at last he wrote to his father, asking permission to enter the navy. It was a manly letter, telling all his reasons for his choice.

The consent was readily given, and Oliver soon afterward received an appointment as midshipman on his father's vessel, the *General Greene*.

IV.—The Cruise in the West Indies.

In the meantime, the people grew more eager for war. An army had been raised to drive back the French, should they attempt to invade the land. George Washington, though nearly sixty-seven years of age, had been appointed commander in chief of the American forces.

In February, 1799, one of the new frigates, the *Constellation*, under Captain Truxton, defeated and captured a French frigate of equal size. By spring the *General Greene* was completed, and Captain Perry was ordered to sail for the West Indies.

CAPT. THOMAS TRUXTON.

America had large trading interests with those islands. Many of our merchant vessels brought from there large cargoes of fruits, coffee, and spices. The *General Greene* was ordered to protect these cargoes from the French cruisers, and bring them safely into port.

For several months Captain Perry's vessel convoyed ships between Cuba and the United States. In July, some of the sailors on board were sick with yellow fever. So Captain Perry brought the vessel back to Newport.

Oliver went at once to see his mother. The tall lad in his bright uniform was a hero to all the children in the neighborhood.

His brothers and sister considered it an honor to wait upon him. They would go out in the early morning and pick berries for his breakfast, so that he might have them with the dew upon them.

While on shipboard he had learned to play a little on the flute. The children loved to sit about him, and listen to his music.

By the autumn of 1799, the crew of the *General Greene* were well again, and Captain Perry sailed back to Havana.

It was during the following winter months of cruising with his father, that Oliver was taught his lessons of naval honor. He also applied the lessons in navigation which he had learned from Mr. Frazer.

He read and studied very carefully, and could not have had a better teacher than his father.

While the *General Greene* was cruising among

the West Indies, Captain Truxton had won
another victory with his *Constellation.* This time
he captured a French frigate which carried sixteen
guns more than the *Constellation.*

The French, dismayed at these victories of the
Americans, began to be more civil. They even
seemed anxious for peace.

THE CONSTELLATION.

War had been carried on for about a year,
though it had never been formally declared.

In May, 1800, the *General Greene* came back to
Newport, and remained in harbor until the terms
of peace were concluded.

The trouble with France being settled, it was

decided by the government to dispose of nearly all the naval vessels. As a result, many of the captains and midshipmen were dismissed, Captain Perry being one of the number.

Fortunately for the country, young Oliver was retained as midshipman.

V.—THE WAR WITH THE BARBARY STATES.

On the northern coast of Africa, bordering on the Mediterranean Sea, are four countries known as the Barbary States. These are Tunis, Algiers, Tripoli, and Morocco.

For more than four hundred years, these countries had been making a business of sea-robbery. Their pirate vessels had seized and plundered the ships of other nations, and the captured officers and men were sold into slavery.

Instead of resisting these robbers, most of the nations had found it easier to pay vast sums of money to the Barbary rulers to obtain protection for their commerce.

The Americans had begun in this way, and had

made presents of money and goods to Algiers and Tunis.

Then the ruler of Tripoli, called the Bashaw, informed our government that he would wait six months for a handsome present from us. If it did not come then, he would declare war against the United States.

This did not frighten the Americans at all. Their only reply was to send a fleet of four vessels to the Mediterranean. The intention was to force the Bashaw to make a treaty which should insure safety for our vessels.

COMMODORE CHARLES MORRIS.

This squadron did not do much but blockade the ports of Tripoli.

A year later, in 1802, a larger squadron was fitted out to bring the Bashaw to terms. Commodore Morris was the commander. On one of the vessels, the *Adams*, was Oliver Perry as midshipman.

Soon after the arrival of his ship in the Mediterranean, Oliver celebrated his seventeenth birthday.

The captain of the *Adams* was very fond of him, and succeeded in having him appointed lieutenant on that day.

For a year and a half, the squadron of Commodore Morris cruised about the Mediterranean. No great battles were fought and no great victories were won.

The *Adams* stopped at the coast towns of Spain, France, and Italy. Through the kindness of the captain, Oliver was often allowed to go on shore and visit the places of interest.

Commodore Morris, being recalled to America, sailed thither in the *Adams;* and so it happened that in November, 1803, Oliver Perry arrived again in America.

His father was then living in Newport, and Oliver remained at home until July of the next year.

He spent much of his time in studying mathematics and astronomy. He liked to go out among the young people, and his pleasing man-

ners and good looks made him a general fa-
vorite.

He was fond of music and could play the flute
very skillfully. When not studying, he liked most
of all to ride horses, and fence with a sword.

While Lieutenant Perry was spending this time
at home, the war in the Mediterranean was still
being carried on. Commodore Preble, who had
succeeded Commodore Morris, had won many
brilliant victories.

The most daring feat of all this war was accomplished by Stephen Decatur, a young lieutenant
only twenty-three years old.

One of the largest of the American vessels, the
Philadelphia, had, by accident, been grounded on
a reef. Taking advantage of her helpless condition,
the whole Tripolitan fleet opened fire upon her.

Captain Bainbridge, the commander of the
Philadelphia, was obliged to surrender. The
Tripolitans managed to float the vessel off the
reef, and towed her into the harbor.

Captain Bainbridge, although a prisoner, found
means to send word of his misfortune to Commo-

dore Preble, who was then at Malta, and the American fleet at once sailed for Tripoli.

At the suggestion of Captain Bainbridge, the Americans determined to burn the *Philadelphia*, rather than allow the Tripolitans to keep her.

This was a very dangerous undertaking, as the vessel was anchored in the midst of the Tripolitan fleet. It was also within easy range of the guns of the fort, commanding the harbor.

The task was given to Stephen Decatur. In order to deceive the enemy, he took a small boat which had been captured from them a short time before. Its crew was made up of volunteers,

STEPHEN DECATUR.

for the chances of escape were very few.

Under cover of night, the little vessel sailed into the harbor, and, as if by accident, ran into the *Philadelphia*. Before the Tripolitans realized what had happened, Decatur and his men were

climbing over the sides of the vessel and through the port holes.

Decatur had ordered his men to use no fire-arms.   He did not wish to attract the attention of

BURNING OF THE PHILADELPHIA

the Tripolitans who were in the fort and on the other vessels in the harbor.

A desperate hand to hand fight ensued.   In a few minutes the Americans were in possession of the vessel.   Some of the Tripolitan crew had been killed; others had jumped into the sea.

The Americans then set the *Philadelphia* on

fire and jumped into their boat to escape. Lieutenant Decatur was the last one to leave the burning ship.

The situation of the little band was now desperate. The *Philadelphia* was a mass of flames, lighting up the harbor for miles around.

Decatur's little boat could be plainly seen, and all the vessels and forts opened fire on it. But the Tripolitans were too much excited to do serious damage.

In a short time the fire reached the magazine of the *Philadelphia* and she blew up with a tremendous crash, leaving the harbor in darkness. Decatur and his men escaped with but one man wounded.

This is only one of many deeds of bravery done in this war, but we can not tell of them in this story. Lieutenant Perry, in his home in America, heard of them, and longed to be on the scene of action.

He was very glad when, in the following September, he was ordered to return in the *Constellation* to the Mediterranean.

The American fleet in the Mediterranean was by this time so large that the Bashaw was convinced that the Americans were in earnest.

He was glad to make a treaty of peace and release the prisoners on payment of a small ransom.

In October, 1806, Oliver Perry returned to America. He was greatly disappointed that he had not been able to take a more active part in the war.

He spent most of the next two years in Newport, dividing his time between study and his many friends.

VI.—MORE TROUBLE WITH ENGLAND.

While America was having these troubles with the Barbary States, France and England were still at war. Commerce all over the world was affected, and in some cases almost destroyed by this long war.

The French emperor, Napoleon Bonaparte, had forbidden all vessels of other nations to enter

British ports. The English, in turn, said that no vessel should enter a port of France, or of any country belonging to France.

But the Americans had to endure still further injuries from the English. British war vessels claimed the right to stop American ships on the sea, search them, and carry off American sailors, claiming them as deserters from the English navy.

The French could not do this ; for no American sailor could be accused of being a runaway Frenchman.

In 1807, an event took place which nearly led to war.

The British frigate *Leopard*, cruising along the coast, hailed the American frigate *Chesapeake*, and demanded permission to search the ship.

The captain of the *Chesapeake* refused. Without a word of warning, the *Leopard* fired into the *Chesapeake*, killing and wounding more than twenty men.

The American captain had not dreamed of such an outrage. His vessel had just put to sea and everything was in confusion. He did not even have a gun in condition to return the fire. So he lowered his flag and surrendered.

The officers of the *Leopard* then came on board and carried off four men from the crew.

The United States would have declared war at once if England had not apologized.

The President, at this time, was Thomas Jefferson. He was a man of peace. He called a session of Congress to see if the trouble could not be settled without war.

As a result of this session, a law was passed known as the Embargo Act. By this law, no vessel was allowed to sail from the United States to any foreign country.

In order to enforce the law, Congress ordered a number of gunboats to be built. These were to sail up and down the coast, and prevent any vessel from entering or leaving the ports.

Lieutenant Perry was ordered to superintend the building of a fleet of these gunboats at Newport. After they were built, he was put in command of them, and ordered to patrol Long Island Sound.

At this time, the government wanted a map of the harbors in the neighborhood of Newport. On account of his standing as a seaman, and of his education, Lieutenant Perry was selected to visit the harbors and make such a map.

He was given a fast sailing schooner called the *Revenge*. While carrying on this work, he was one day returning from Newport to New London, when a dense fog came on. The *Revenge* struck upon a reef of rocks, and went to pieces.

By great efforts Lieutenant Perry was able to save, not only all the crew, but the sails, rigging, and cannon.

He then went to Washington to explain the loss of the *Revenge* to the navy department. It was made clear that it was the fault of the local pilot who had charge of the vessel at the time.

Lieutenant Perry was commended for his gallant conduct in this disaster, and was also granted a year's leave of absence. He went to Newport, and on May 5, 1811, he was married to Elizabeth Champlin Mason.

The young couple took a wedding journey

through New England. They spent one day in
Plymouth, Massachusetts. Lieutenant Perry was
much interested in visiting the place where his
Quaker ancestor had lived so many years before.

During this time, the people of the United
States had learned that the Embargo Act was a
very unwise law. The men of Congress had
thought to injure France and England by thus re-
fusing to trade with them altogether. They soon
discovered, however, that the dam-
age to American commerce was far
greater.

Trading vessels in the ports were
left standing idle at the wharves,
while the sailors were forced to find
other employment.

JAMES MADISON.

All over the country, there arose a bitter feeling
against this law. In the New England states,
where there were the largest shipping interests,
there was even talk of secession from the Union.

About this time a new President, James Madison,
was elected. Soon afterward the Embargo Act
was repealed, and in its place was passed a law

which satisfied the people for a time. By this law, trade was allowed with every country but England and France.

American vessels now put to sea on voyages to foreign lands. But their old enemies, the English, soon began to annoy them as before.

In May, 1811, the British sloop *Little Belt* was hailed by the American frigate *President*, under the command of Commodore Rodgers. The reply was a cannon shot. The *President* then poured broadsides into the *Little Belt*. After the English had lost thirty-two men in killed and wounded, they came to terms.

COMMODORE JOHN RODGERS.

The American people now saw that war could no longer be avoided. On June 18, 1812. the formal declaration was made.

VII.—WAR ON THE CANADIAN BORDER.

Up to this time the English navy had been called the "Mistress of the Seas." England's vessels could be numbered by the hundred, and the crews by the ten thousand.

When this war of 1812 was declared, the entire United States navy comprised about half a dozen frigates, and six or eight sloops and brigs. Along the American coast alone the English had seven times this number of war vessels.

The first few months of the war were full of naval surprises. In that brief time the Americans captured more British ships than the French had taken in twenty years.

On August 19th, the American frigate *Constitution*, commanded by Captain Isaac Hull, in one half hour captured the English frigate *Guerrière*. The English lost one hundred men, and the vessel was so disabled that she was left to sink. The Americans lost but fourteen men, and in a few hours the ship was ready for another battle.

Several other victories followed in quick succession. In all this time the Americans did not lose a ship.

In December, Commodore Bainbridge, the same officer who had been taken prisoner years before by the Tripolitans and had afterwards been promoted, was cruising with the frigate *Constitution* off the coast of Brazil. He there encountered and captured the British frigate *Java*.

But though so successful on the sea, the Americans were defeated many times on land.

The possession of the Great Lakes was of the utmost importance to both the English and the Americans.

Ever since the Revolution the English had kept a naval force on these lakes. They had hoped that some time they might be able to extend the Canadian territory along the Great Lakes and down the Mississippi to New Orleans. This would give them the possession of the great west.

Many prosperous towns and trading posts were scattered along the Canadian shores. To capture some of these was the task given to the American army.

The campaign was opened by General William Hull. With two thousand men he crossed the Detroit River, and marched into Canada.

After a few skirmishes with the Indians, he fell back to the fort at Detroit. Then, without firing a single gun, he gave up this fort to the English. This surrender was a great loss to the Americans for many reasons.

There was, in the west, a bold Indian warrior whose name was Tecumseh. He had a brother whom the Indians called the Prophet, because he was a medicine man and could do wonderful things.

These two Indians wished to form a union of all the tribes from Canada to the Gulf of Mexico. They hoped that in this way they might prevent the white settlers from taking their hunting grounds.

TECUMSEH.

"The white men are continually driving the red

people toward the west ; by and by we shall be driven into the Great Water," they said.

The governor-general of Canada made the Indians many promises, and tried to incite them against the United States. In this way he persuaded many warlike tribes to give aid to the English. Tecumseh himself crossed into Canada and joined the British army under General Proctor.

After Hull's surrender of Detroit, the British and Indians took possession not only of that fort, but also of Fort Dearborn, where Chicago now stands. The territory of Michigan was completely in their hands, and the settlers along the lakes and all through the northwest were at the mercy of the Indians.

General William Henry Harrison tried to regain Detroit. His advance guard was met and defeated at the River Raisin, a few

WILLIAM HENRY
HARRISON.

miles south of Detroit. Every American prisoner was murdered by the Indians; and for years afterward the River Raisin was a name of horror.

The Americans felt that something desperate must be done. The first great thing to be gained was the control of the lakes.

At this time nearly the whole of the western country was a wilderness. The only way of moving men and supplies from place to place, was by the use of boats on the lakes and water courses.

On Lake Ontario a small fleet had been built, and a skirmish or two had been fought. But the thing of most importance was the control of Lake Erie. This would not only give back Detroit to the Americans, but would also be the means of recovering the whole of the Michigan territory.

The task of building a fleet and driving the English from the lakes was given to Lieutenant Perry.

At the beginning of the war he had left his quiet home in Newport, and had hurried to Washington to ask for active service.

He was promised the first vacancy, but in the meantime he was ordered to protect the harbors of Long Island Sound with a flotilla of gunboats.

During the year 1812 he performed this duty

faithfully, all the while drilling his men, in hopes of being intrusted with a larger responsibility.

VIII.—OLIVER PERRY BUILDS A FLEET.

In February, 1813, Lieutenant Perry was ordered to go to Lake Erie. He was to take with him, from his gunboats, the men whom he thought best fitted for the service and report to Commodore Chauncey, who was in command of the squadron on Lake Ontario. The American headquarters, on that lake, were at Sacketts Harbor.

It was almost impossible to reach the place. From the Hudson River to the shores of Lake Ontario, was a vast wilderness. No road had been cut through it; none but Indians could follow the difficult trails.

The only route known to the white men was along the Mohawk River to Lake Oneida, then by the Oswego River to the little village of Oswego on Lake Ontario. To transport men and arms along this route was a great task, requiring much time, skill, and patience.

Oliver Perry was a man of action. On the very day that he received his orders, he started fifty men to Lake Ontario, and the next day fifty more.

On February 22d, in the coldest part of winter, he left his home and his young wife in Newport,

and with his brother Alexander, began the difficult journey towards the north.

Sometimes they traveled in rude sleighs over the roughest of roads. Sometimes, when the river was not too full of ice, they embarked in canoes. At other times, they could only go on foot through the thick underbrush. On all sides was a vast wilderness, inhabited only by wild beasts and unfriendly Indians.

At Oswego, they embarked in boats and followed the shore of Lake Ontario to Sacketts Harbor. On one side of them was the dreary inland sea full of tossing white caps and overhung by the leaden sky of winter. On the other side lay the trackless forest.

To relieve their loneliness, they occasionally fired a musket. The echoes would roll along the shore, growing fainter and fainter. This only made the silence which followed seem greater than before.

A cold rain began to fall, and by the time they reached Sacketts Harbor they were drenched to the skin.

On March 16th, Lieutenant Perry set out for Lake Erie. Upon reaching the harbor at Erie he found that twenty-five ship carpenters had already begun work on three gunboats and two brigs. Fifty more carpenters had started four weeks before from Philadelphia, but had not yet arrived.

The task which lay before Oliver Perry seemed almost an impossible one. Mechanics, seamen, guns, sailcloth,—everything needed for the ships must be brought hundreds of miles through a wild and half-settled country.

But by the end of the summer, a fleet, which seemed to have been built by magic, was ready to meet the English. Six months before, the timbers used in building the vessels had been growing trees; the iron that held these timbers together was either in the mines or in warehouses or farmers' barns, in the shape of plowshares, axes, or horseshoes.

The shipbuilders had come through the wilderness from Philadelphia. The guns, ammunition, and rigging had been brought in ox-wagons, hundreds of miles over almost impassable roads.

While Perry was building this fleet, a sad event had taken place on the sea. The British frigate *Shannon* met and captured the American frigate *Chesapeake*, June 1, 1813, near Boston harbor.

CAPTAIN JAMES LAWRENCE.

Captain Lawrence of the *Chesapeake* fought bravely, but, in the battle, was mortally wounded. As he was being

carried below, his last words were: " Don't give up the ship ! "

The Secretary of the Navy sent word to Lieutenant Perry to name one of the vessels of his new fleet the *Lawrence*, after this gallant captain. Lieutenant Perry therefore gave this name to his flagship.

By the 10th of July the fleet was ready for sea, but there were only officers and men enough to man one ship. Several of these were ill with fever.

Lieutenant Perry wrote many letters to General Harrison, Commodore Chauncey, and the Secretary of the Navy.

"Give me men, and I will acquire both for you and for myself honor and glory on this lake, or die in the attempt." he said.

By the end of July he had over four hundred men for his nine vessels. But, as he said, they were a "motley crew" of regular soldiers, negroes, and raw recruits. During the battle which followed, over a hundred of these men were too sick to be of any use.

The English fleet of six vessels was commanded

by Captain Barclay.   In his crews were over five hundred men and boys.

IX.—"We Have Met the Enemy and They are Ours."

Early in August the American squadron left the harbor of Erie, and sailed to Put-in-Bay, an island not far from the west end of the lake.

The British squadron was in the harbor of Fort Malden, nearly opposite on the Canadian shore.

On the morning of September 10, 1813, from the masthead of the *Lawrence*, the English fleet was seen approaching.

As the Americans were sailing out to battle, Lieutenant Perry gathered his men together and talked to them about the courage they would need.

He showed them a large blue flag, bearing in white letters a foot high the words: "Don't give up the ship!"

"My brave lads," he said, "this flag bears the last words of Captain Lawrence.   Shall I hoist it?"

With one voice, the men shouted: "Aye, aye, sir!"

As the bunting was run up on the *Lawrence*, cheer upon cheer came from every vessel of the American squadron. The men were then sent to their quarters, and every one quietly waited for the beginning of battle.

It was a beautiful morning. The sky was cloudless, and there was hardly a ripple to disturb the lake. The English vessels were newly painted, and gayly adorned with flags. Every sail shone in dazzling whiteness in the sunlight.

At half-past ten a bugle was heard from the English flagship, which was followed by cheers from the other vessels. Across the water the Americans could hear the strains of the English national air played by a band.

On the *Lawrence* all was still. With determined faces the men stood by the guns.

Lieutenant Perry knew that a great responsibility was upon him. He knew that, should he lose the battle, General Proctor and Tecumseh, with five thousand soldiers and Indians, were ready to

cross the lake, and take possession of the southern
shore. All through that part of the country,
anxious men, women, and children were waiting
to flee from their homes, if the dreaded Indians
came upon them.

These things Lieutenant Perry knew. He
passed along the deck, carefully examining every
gun. He had a word of encouragement for each
gun crew.

Seeing some of the men who had fought on the
Constitution, he said, "I need not say anything to
you. You know how to beat those fellows."

As he passed another gun, commanded by a crew
that had served in his gunboat flotilla, he said:
"Here are the Newport boys! They will do their
duty, I warrant."

In this way he filled all his men with a great
earnestness, and a determination to conquer or die.

While the two squadrons were yet a mile apart,
the English sent a cannon ball skimming over the
water. For some time there followed a vigorous
firing from both sides.

As the English guns could carry farther than

those of the Americans, Lieutenant Perry brought his flagship into close quarters. The other American vessels were some distance behind.

The whole British squadron then opened fire upon the *Lawrence.*

At the end of an hour of this unequal battle, the condition of the *Lawrence* was pitiable. One by one the guns had been disabled. Finally only one on the side toward the enemy could be used. The rigging was damaged, the spars were shattered, and the sails were torn into shreds. Eighty-three men had been killed or wounded.

Two musket balls passed through Lieutenant Perry's hat, and his clothing was torn by flying splinters.

One heavy shot crushed into the large china closet, and smashed every dish with a great clatter. A dog, that had been locked up there, startled by the noise, added to the tumult by howling dismally.

Several times the *Lawrence* barely escaped being blown up. Two cannon balls passed entirely through the powder magazine.

Even the wounded men crawled upon the deck
to lend a feeble hand in firing the guns. It was
Oliver Perry himself, however, that loaded and
fired the last gun of the *Lawrence*.

Lieutenant Perry at last determined to change
his flag from the *Lawrence* to the *Niagara*. A
breeze had sprung up, which enabled this vessel to
come near to the helpless *Lawrence*.

The first lieutenant was left in command of the
Lawrence, with orders to hold out to the last.
Then with his brother Alexander and four seamen,
Lieutenant Perry got into a rowboat. Just as
they were shoving off, a seaman on the *Lawrence*
hauled down the blue flag, bearing the motto,
"Don't give up the ship!" He rolled it up and
tossed it to Perry.

The smoke of the battle was so dense that the
rowboat had nearly reached the *Niagara* before it
was seen by the English. Then a shot was sent
which went straight through the boat's side.

Taking off his coat and rolling it up, Perry
quickly thrust it into the hole which the ball had
made. This kept the boat from sinking.

As he stepped upon the deck of the *Niagara*,
Perry ordered the blue flag to be hoisted. Just at
this moment the *Lawrence* surrendered.

The English gave a cheer, thinking they had
won the battle. They were not able, however, to

THE BATTLE OF LAKE ERIE.

board and take the *Lawrence* at once, and so she
drifted away. When safely out of range her
colors were rehoisted.

Bringing the *Niagara* into position, Lieutenant
Perry fired a terrific broadside into one of the English vessels. Then he sailed quickly to another
and did the same thing.

The other American vessels followed this exam-
ple, and a terrific battle followed.

In just fifteen minutes the English surrendered. Two vessels of their squadron attempted to escape, but were soon overtaken and captured.

Lieutenant Perry was determined that the formal surrender should take place on the *Lawrence.* So once more he lowered his flag, and jumping into a boat, made for his first flagship.

When he stepped on board the *Lawrence* not a cheer was heard. The handful of men that were left silently greeted their commander.

Few of them were uninjured. Some had splintered arms and legs. Others had bandages about their heads. Their faces were black with powder.

The English officers came on board to present their swords to Perry. With quiet dignity he returned each one.

He then took from his pocket an old letter. Using his cap for a desk, he wrote with a pencil his famous dispatch to General Harrison:

"We have met the enemy and they are ours. Two ships, two brigs, one schooner, and one sloop. Yours, with very great respect and esteem,

"O. H. PERRY."

X.—What Perry's Victory Accomplished.

The battle on Lake Erie was the beginning of the end of the war. The news of the victory caused great rejoicings all over the country. In all the principal towns there were meetings, bonfires, and torchlight processions.

General Harrison could now take his army into Canada. No time was lost. He hurried over four thousand men to the lake, where Perry's fleet waited to take them across.

The main body of the British army, under General Proctor and Tecumseh, was at Fort Malden. Upon landing there the Americans found that the enemy had fled, having burned the forts, barracks, and stores.

General Harrison followed the English up the left bank of the Detroit River. The fort at Detroit was surrendered without any resistance, and the English retreated along the St. Clair Lake and up the Thames River.

The Americans steadily pursued them. Perry,

with his fleet, followed the army, carrying the baggage and provisions.

He became so excited over the chase that he could not remain quietly on his ships. So, leaving them in charge of one of his officers, he went ashore and offered his services to General Harrison as aid-de-camp.

As he joined the army he was met with cheers of welcome from the soldiers. General Harrison afterward said : "The appearance of the gallant Perry cheered and animated every soldier."

Following the English some distance up the Thames, the Americans finally overtook them. They were drawn up in line of battle on a narrow strip of land which lay between the river and a large swamp.

The American cavalry made a bold dash through these lines, and the enemy was soon routed. Over sixty British and Indians were killed, and six hundred troops were made prisoners. General Proctor made his escape, but Tecumseh was killed.

The death of this great chief severed forever the

tie which bound the Indians to the English. Soon
afterwards all the tribes of the northwest declared
submission to the United States. The white settlers in the region about the Great Lakes were
thus freed from their fear of the savages.

During the battle of the Thames, the soldiers
greatly admired the fine horsemanship of Oliver
Perry. He rode a powerful black horse, with a
white face, that could be seen from all parts of the
field.

Once, when riding swiftly to carry out some orders
of the general's, the horse plunged into the deep
mire to his breast. Perry pressed his hands on
the pommel of the saddle, and sprang over the
horse's head to dry ground.

Relieved from the weight of his rider, the
horse freed himself and bounded forward. Perry
clutched the mane as he passed and vaulted into
the saddle, without stopping the animal's speed for
a moment. As he passed the soldiers, many
cheers arose.

On October 7, 1813, Perry returned to Detroit,
and from there started back to his home in New-

port. The people hailed him with joy, and enough could not be said in his praises. Even Captain Barclay of the English fleet called him "The gallant and generous enemy."

His journey to Newport was indeed a triumphal one. In every town that he passed through, business was stopped and the schools were closed so that all could have a glimpse of the hero of Lake Erie. Processions accompanied him from town to town.

On November 18th, he reached his home in Newport. Bells were rung, all the ships were adorned with flags, and salutes were fired in his honor.

GOLD MEDAL AWARDED BY CONGRESS.

On November 29th, he received his promotion to the rank of captain. At that time this was the highest rank in the American navy. A gold medal was also given to him by Congress.

In the following January he made a visit to Washington, where he was publicly entertained by the President and citizens.

In August, 1814, he was ordered to command a new frigate named the *Java*. He hastened to Baltimore, where this vessel was to be launched.

On the 11th of September, Lieutenant Macdonough, who was in command of the American squadron on Lake Champlain, gained a decisive victory over the British near Plattsburg. Everything at the North seemed now to be favorable to the Americans; but it was not so at the South.

While Captain Perry was waiting at Baltimore, the British had sailed up the Potomac with an army and a fleet. They captured Washington, and burned the capitol, the White House, and some of the other public buildings.

Being so successful in this, they made a like attempt upon Baltimore, but were driven back. They then blockaded Chesapeake Bay.

Just at this time, Congress passed a bill to fit out two squadrons of fast-sailing vessels. These were to cruise near the English coasts and destroy the commerce between the different ports.

Captain Perry was ordered to leave the *Java* and command one of these squadrons. But before he could sail for England, peace was declared. A treaty with that country was signed December 24, 1814.

XI.—ON THE MEDITERRANEAN AGAIN.

While the United States had been at war with England, trouble had again arisen with the Barbary States. None of these countries had been so annoying as Algiers. The ruler, or Dey, of Algiers knew that every American naval vessel was busy fighting the English. He therefore thought this a good time to burn and plunder the merchant ships. He also demanded large sums of money in return for his captured prizes and prisoners.

But no sooner was peace concluded with England, than Congress declared war with Algiers. A squadron was sent to the Mediterranean, commanded by the brave Stephen Decatur, and he soon compelled the Dey to sign a treaty with the United States.

In this treaty the Dey promised to give back all the American property he had captured. If there was anything that he could not return, he was to pay for it at its full value. He was also to release all the Americans he held as prisoners, and give up, forever, all claim to tribute money from the United States.

When the consuls of other countries heard of what Decatur had accomplished, they tried to persuade the Algerine ruler to make the same terms with them. Then the Dey was sorry that he had "humbled himself" before the young republic, and he declared that he did not consider the treaty binding.

Congress therefore thought it wise to strengthen the American squadron in the Mediterranean, in order that this trouble should be settled.

Captain Perry was ordered to take the *Java* and sail at once for Algiers. On January 22, 1816, he set sail, and in March he joined the American vessels off the eastern coast of Spain.

Upon arriving at Algiers, they found that the Dey had just received a large amount of tribute money from an English fleet. This made him very unwilling to talk about treaties.

The English fleet had not only brought money to pay for the release of English prisoners, but also had brought vast sums from the governments of Naples and Sardinia to buy the freedom of their enslaved countrymen.

Twelve hundred captives were freed in this way, and put aboard the English vessels. There were people of all ages, clothed in rags. Some had been taken while young and now were old men, with gray hair and beards.

The Dey refused to treat with the American commander, and the Americans would have destroyed the Algerian fleet and bombarded the town at once, but for an article in the treaty which Decatur had made. This article stated that when either side should become dissatisfied with the treaty, three months' notice should be given before actual fighting began.

While waiting for these three months to pass,

the American squadron cruised about the Mediterranean and visited the other Barbary States. The commander wished to show the rulers of these states that our country had a navy which could protect our commerce.

After this the fleet sailed along the southern coast of Europe. There was no vessel which attracted more admiration than Captain Perry's *Java*. To visit this ship was, indeed, a pleasure.

The captain was a courteous host, and always made his guests welcome. Everything on the ship was in order, and ready for instant use. The discipline of the crew was perfect.

Being a good musician himself, Captain Perry had the finest band in all the fleet. He took a personal interest in each one of his men, and was always ready with a word of praise when he saw it was deserved. He gave the midshipmen lessons in navigation, and saw that they had lessons in Spanish and French and in the use of the sword. They were even taught to dance.

Whenever it was possible the men were allowed

to go on shore, in order that they might visit the
places of interest.

By January, 1817, the Dey of Algiers finally
came to terms and signed a new treaty, agreeing
to the conditions required by the United States.
Captain Perry was soon afterwards ordered to
sail for America, carrying this new treaty with
him. In March he arrived at Newport.

XII.—Captain Perry's Last Cruise.

After so many months of cruising, Captain Perry
was very glad to be again in his own country.

He spent the next two years quietly at home
with his family. He built a snug little cottage in
Narragansett, on the old Perry estate. This was
the same farm that had been purchased by the
young Quaker, Edmund Perry, so many years
before. Here the family spent the summers.

Captain Perry was always fond of life in the
country. He took many long rides on horseback.
Besides his horses, he had many other pets on the

farm. He and his three little sons spent a great
deal of time taking care of them.

The winters were passed in the house at
Newport.

These were the happiest years of Oliver Perry's
life, and he could not help but be sorry, when, on

CAPTAIN PERRY'S RESIDENCE AT NEWPORT.

March 31, 1819, he received a summons to go to
Washington.

Upon arriving there, the Secretary of the Navy
told him of an expedition that the government
wished him to undertake.

He was to go to Venezuela, on the northern
coast of South America. This was a new republic

which had formerly been a colony of Spain. Its people were still fighting for their independence, just as the people of the United States had fought against the king of England.

Small, fast-sailing war vessels, called privateers, had been fitted out by this republic. These vessels were designed to capture Spanish merchant ships, and were allowed to keep all the money that was obtained from the prizes.

But it was not the Spanish ships alone which suffered from these privateers. The desire for prize money led them to attack ships of other nations. The American merchants had met with many losses in this way.

Captain Perry was to present claims for these losses, and also to persuade the president of Venezuela to keep his privateers from preying on American commerce. For this expedition, Perry was to have two vessels, the sloop *John Adams* and the schooner *Nonsuch*.

On July 15, 1817, he arrived at the mouth of the Orinoco River. Here he was obliged to take the small schooner in order to go up the river and

reach the town of Angostura, which was then the
Venezuelan capital. He sent the *John Adams* to
Port Spain, on the island of Trinidad, one hundred and fifty miles away. This vessel was ordered to wait there for his return.

The voyage up the Orinoco was an interesting
one. All along the shores were vast tropical for-
ests with overhanging trees full of birds of brilliant
colors. Luxuriant vines were festooned from limb
to limb. Flowers of all colors grew everywhere.

On the other hand, the trip was full of hardships.
The heat was fearful and the sand-flies, gnats,
and mosquitoes were almost unbearable.

Soon after reaching Angostura many of the
crew were taken ill with yellow fever, but Perry
would not leave until his mission was accomplished. After three weeks of delay, he succeeded
in getting the promises for which he had come.

The schooner then sailed down the river, reaching the mouth on August 15th. On account of a
high sea, to cross the bar that night would be a
dangerous undertaking, and the vessel was therefore anchored until morning.

During the night, the wind freshened so much that the spray dashed into the cabin where Captain Perry was sleeping.   In the morning he awoke with a cold chill and symptoms of yellow fever.

Every effort was made to reach the *John Adams* as soon as possible.   Captain Perry grew rapidly worse.   In the intense heat, his little schooner cabin was most uncomfortable.

The winds were unfavorable and the progress of the little vessel was slow.   When within a mile of the *John Adams*, Captain Perry died.   This was on his thirty-fourth birthday, August 23, 1819.

He was buried on the island of Trinidad with military honors, and the *John Adams* brought back the sad news to the United States.

His death was regarded as a national calamity. The government sent a war vessel to bring his body home.   He was finally laid to rest at Newport, where a granite monument marks his grave.

The feelings of his fellow officers were well expressed by Stephen Decatur.   Upon hearing of Perry's death, he said: "Sir! The American navy has lost its brightest ornament!"